A POCKET GUIDE TO RUNES

by Ben Waggoner

The Troth
Philadelphia
2019

© 2019, The Troth. All rights reserved. No part of this book may be reproduced or transmitted in any form or by any means, electronic or mechanical, including photocopy, recording, or any information storage and retrieval system, without prior permission in writing from the publisher. Exceptions may be allowed for non-commercial "fair use," for the purposes of news reporting, criticism, comment, scholarship, research, or teaching.

Published by The Troth
325 Chestnut Street, Suite 800
Philadelphia, PA 19106
http://www.thetroth.org/

ISBN-13: 978-1-941136-25-6 (paperback)
978-1-941136-26-3 (PDF e-book)

Troth logo designed by Kveldúlfr Gundarsson; drawn by 13 Labs, Chicago, Illinois. Cover designed by Ben Waggoner. Cover images courtesy of the Swedish Historical Museum; cover textures courtesy of Freepik.com.

Special thanks to Perseus Greenman, Dara Grey, Kveldulf Gundarsson, Scott Mohnkern, Diana Paxson, and Ben Waggoner for their helpful comments and critiques.

Rune	Name	Meaning	Letter
ᚠ	*fehu*	wealth/cattle	f
ᚢ	*uruz*	aurochs	u
ᚦ	*thurisaz*	giant	th
ᚨ	*ansuz*	Æsir god	a
ᚱ	*raidho*	riding	r
ᚲ	*kenaz*	torch	k
ᚷ	*gebo*	gift	g
ᚹ	*wunjo*	joy	w
ᚺ	*hagalaz*	hail	h
ᚾ	*naudhiz*	need	n
ᛁ	*isa*	ice	i
ᛃ	*jera*	year/harvest	y
ᛇ	*eiwaz*	yew	ï
ᛈ	*perthro*	dice-cup	p
ᛉ	*elhaz*	elk	-z, -r
ᛋ	*sowilo*	sun	s
ᛏ	*tiwaz*	Tyr	t
ᛒ	*berkano*	birch	b
ᛖ	*ehwaz*	horse	e
ᛗ	*mannaz*	man	m
ᛚ	*laguz*	lake	l
ᛜ	*ingwaz*	Ing	-ng
ᛞ	*dagaz*	day	d
ᛟ	*othala*	estate	o

What are runes?

The word *rune* originally meant "secret" or "mystery" in the Germanic languages—it's related to the German word *raunen* and the archaic English word *to roun*, both meaning "to whisper; to murmur." It is also related to words for "counsel" or "advice." For example, the Old English poem *The Wanderer* contains the lines *Swa cwæð snottor on mode, gesæt him sundor æt rune*—"So spoke the wise man in his mind; he sat apart **taking counsel**."

The word *rune* came to be applied to the letters that were used to write various Germanic languages, such as late Proto-Germanic, Gothic, Old Norse, and Old English, between about 200 and 1400 CE. These letters were originally called "rune-staves" (*rūn-stafas* in Old English, *rúna-stafi* in Old Norse). Today, the letters are commonly called "runes" for short.

Those who work with runes in magic today often consider a rune, on the most esoteric level, to be a mystery of the cosmos, manifesting throughout the world and in human life. A rune is also the sign and the sounds which represent the mystery, through which the mystery can be understood and worked with.

Why do rune letters have such angular shapes?

The angular appearance of the rune letters probably stems from the fact that they were originally designed to be carved on wood or stone. Curved lines are difficult to carve, and horizontal cuts are likely to blend into the grain of a piece of wood (and possibly split the wood), and so the letters are primarily made up of vertical and diagonal strokes. Some wooden objects with carved runes have survived, but most rune inscriptions that have come down to us were carved or stamped on more durable materials, such as stone, bone, or metal. Carved runes were often colored or stained with blood or paint. Medieval manuscripts written in part or completely in runes have also come down to us.

For what purposes were runes used?

Rune letters were and are used in the same ways as any writing system. Messages of all kinds, from business letters and Christian poetry to love charms and obscene graffiti, have been found written in runes on early medieval artifacts. Runes were widely used in Scandinavia and Britain for memorial inscriptions, even well after the introduction of the Latin alphabet and the coming of Christianity. Even completely Christian texts could be carved in runes—such as the Ruthwell Cross from southern Scotland, which is carved with lines from the pious Christian poem *The Dream of the Rood*. A number of amulets excavated at Bryggen, in Bergen, Norway, dating as late as the 14th century, bear rune inscriptions that invoke Jesus and Mary for protection. Just because something is written in runes does not automatically make it "pagan", magical, or mystical in any way.

However, perhaps the most famous historical use of runes, if not necessarily the most common, was in magical practices, both before and after the adoption of Christianity in northern Europe. Both artifacts and literary references show that runes were carved on amulets, weapons, and other gear, for protection, healing, good fortune, blessing, or cursing. There is indirect evidence for the use of rune sounds in chanted magic (*galdor*). Rune letters were probably also used in divination: the 9th-century German bishop Hrabanus Maurus wrote, "Those whom we call heathens use these letters to record their poems, magical songs and predictions." Heathens today still use runes for all of these purposes.

Is there a blank rune?
No. The blank rune is a modern invention.

Are runes different from other ancient alphabets and divination systems?
Runes are sometimes confused with *ogham*, an alphabet used by the Irish and other Celtic peoples (also called the Beth-Luis-Nin alphabet, after the names of the first three letters). However, the shapes and meanings of the ogham letters are quite different from those of the runes. The letters used to write Old Turkic inscriptions in the 8th–10th centuries, and Old Hungarian beginning in the 10th century, are sometimes called "runes" and look somewhat similar to the Germanic runes. However, they are used to write very different languages.

Some recent writers have tried to link runes with the Kabbalistic Tree of Sephiroth, or the Tarot, or the Hebrew alphabet, or the I Ching. Most runemasters today would agree that there's no need to do this: we have enough knowledge about how the runes were used in ancient times to recreate a free-standing system of knowledge. Other modern writers have developed systems of correspondences between runes and gemstones, herbs, or constellations. While there is no documented basis for these systems, they should be evaluated on their own merits, through experience.

How did the runes originate?

In the mundane sense, the rune letters were probably derived from an alphabet used in north Italy that was derived from a version of the Greek alphabet, related to the Etruscan alphabet and the Latin alphabet (which were also derived from a variant of the Greek alphabet). This explains why many rune letters look like angular versions of our own. Some letters were added or modified to express sounds found only in Germanic. A helmet found in Negau, in what is now Slovenia, bears an inscription in the Etruscan alphabet made before 50 BCE; it contains the Germanic personal name Harigast ("army guest"). This suggests that some Germanic-speaking people knew the Etruscan alphabet and could write their own language in it. The runes may have originated from this practice, although scholars still debate the matter.

The oldest inscription in runelike letters from the German-speaking regions—four letters on a cloak pin found near Meldorf, Germany—date from about the year 50 CE. More certain rune inscriptions, on artifacts form Vimose, Denmark, may be as old as 160 CE. The oldest complete rune alphabet (*futhark*), carved on the Kylver stone from the island of Gotland in Sweden, dates to about 400 CE.

Before the invention of the runes, Scandinavian people in the Bronze Age and Iron Age carved symbols on stones, probably for ritual or magical purposes. These signs are called *hällristningar* in modern Swedish. Some of these shapes resemble rune letters, and it's possible that their shapes and meanings influenced the shapes and meaning of the runes.

What is a futhark?

A futhark is a rune alphabet. Just as the word "alphabet" comes from the names of the first two Greek letters, *alpha* and *beta*, the word "futhark" comes from the first six rune letters, with the sounds **f**, **u**, **th**, **a**, **r**, and **k**. Different futharks were used at different times and places, but all begin with these six letters.

Elder Futhark carved on the Kylver Stone, Gotland, Sweden, ca. 400 CE. Some rune letters are incomplete.

This booklet focuses on the oldest rune alphabet, the Elder Futhark of twenty-four letters. This futhark was used in Germany and Scandinavia until about 600 AD. Later futharks added, changed or deleted various letters. Shifts in the sounds of certain letters explain why the Anglo-Saxon or Anglo-Frisian rune alphabet is technically a *futhorc*. The Anglo-Saxon Futhorc has twenty-nine letters (later expanded to thirty-three in northern England), some of which represented sounds that were unique to the Old English language. The various Scandinavian or Younger Futharks, used by the Vikings among others, contain only sixteen rune letters, some of which developed simplified shapes. This reduction meant that several letters had to represent multiple sounds: the **b** rune also represented **p**, the **u** rune also represented **o** and **w**, and so on. The Anglo-Saxon Futhorc (top) and the Danish version of the Younger Futhark (bottom) are shown here.

Incidentally, J.R.R. Tolkien—a professor of Old English who knew the runes well—used English runes in *The Hobbit*. In *The Lord of the Rings*, he developed his own rune alphabet, the *Cirth*, which looks much like historical runes, but is quite different in detail from the ones that were used by the historical Germanic-speaking peoples.

Weren't runes used by the Nazis?

The German Nazi Party tried to appeal to a sense of "Germanic" identity by using ancient symbols for their own propagandistic purposes. The swastika was the best-known of those symbols, but some rune letters were used as well, notably the *elhaz* rune ("protection"), the *othala* rune ("ancestral property"), and the *sowilo* rune ("sun"), which was doubled to produce the emblem of the SS. Regrettably, some modern "white nationalist" and neo-Nazi groups use rune letters as emblems and symbols as well. The Troth—the organization that publishes this booklet—has no sympathy whatsoever with such ideologies, and considers this use of runes to be a tragic and foolish misuse of a cultural tradition. There is no support for racial or ethnic hatred or supremacy in the old myths or lore.

What are the Armanen runes?

The Armanen runes were originated by the Austrian writer and occultist Guido List. He allegedly saw the runes in a mystical vision while temporarily blind, recovering from cataract surgery in 1902. His version of the futhark is much like the Younger Futhark, but with two runes added to represent **e** and **g**. List felt that these runes had been used by an ancient German priesthood, the Armanen. List's runes are still popular in some occult circles, but they are not identical with any known historical futhark. List made these runes part of a religious and magical system called Armanism, supposedly practiced by ancient German priest-kings. There is no evidence that such a priesthood existed, and unfortunately, some of List's ideas were adopted by the Nazis, notably Heinrich Himmler.

What are the ætts?

Ætt means "clan" or "tribe" in Norse. Traditionally, the futhark is divided into three ætts or *ættir*, a division seen on some of the oldest artifacts, such as the Vadstena *bracteate* (sheet gold medallion) shown on the cover of this booklet. In the Elder Futhark, each ætt consists of eight runes. Some Heathens call the first eight runes Frey's Ætt, the second eight Hagal's or Heimdall's Ætt, and the last eight Tyr's Ætt. Some rune-workers feel that runes in the same ætt are meaningfully connected. Others disagree—this is an area in which you should work to develop your own understanding.

How are runes used in divination?

The Roman author Tacitus described ancient German divination. The diviner cut slips of wood from a fruit-bearing tree, marked them with distinguishing signs (*notae*, in Latin), and tossed the slips onto a white cloth. Then he would take up three of the slips and interpret their meaning. Tacitus didn't describe the "signs", but some scholars think that they were runes or rune-like symbols. The Rune Poems are thought to contain clues to the meanings of the runes in divination. The poem *Hávamál*, "Speech of the High One," preserved in the collection now called the *Poetic Edda*, mentions the process of "asking the runes," although the verse may refer to runes as mysteries, not as letters.

Today, rune-lots (rune letters used for divination) may be drawn on cards, modeled in ceramics, or carved into pieces of wood, stone, glass or metal. Sets of runes can be purchased, but some feel that the best set of rune-lots is the one that a caster makes himself or herself. The simplest way of divination is to meditate on a question and then draw three runes at random, similar to the procedure described by Tacitus. The first rune that is drawn is usually thought to represent factors in the past that are contributing to the situation at hand. The second rune represents the current "state of affairs." The third rune represents what would be expected to result if action to change it is not taken, growing out of the present situation and its past influences. However, the third rune does not represent unalterable fate.

More complex divination "spreads" are used by some modern runeworkers, some of which have been inspired by Tarot card spreads. Some runecasters read runes using the principle of inversion: a rune that appears upside-down in a divinatory spread represents an inversion or blockage of what it would mean appearing right side up. Others don't believe that inversion is important—nine of the runes look the same whether inverted or not, anyway. Some runecasters use the position of the runes with respect to each other to distinguish between positive and negative aspects (sometimes called *bright-staves* and *mirk-staves*, or *bjartstafir* and *myrkstafir* in Old Norse). Yet another method of divination is to carve runes on long sticks, let them fall at random, and interpret the positions and crossings of the sticks. This is a complex subject; if you study rune divination further, keep records and find out what gives you the best results.

How are runes used in talismanic magic?

Any rune or combination of runes may be engraved on an object that the runemaster carries or gives to someone else. The power of the rune is "loaded" into the object by the act of carving, by the runecarver's songs or spells (*galdor*), and usually by inlaying color into the rune as well. Traditionally, runes are colored red, whether with blood or with other natural red pigments such as ochre.

One of the most powerful kinds of magic in Viking times was the *niðstöng*, the "pole of insult"—a pole topped with a horse's head, set up facing the victim's home, with a curse formula (*formáli*) carved on it in runes. The Icelandic *Egil's Saga* describes a famous instance of raising a *niðstöng*. *Grettir's Saga* describes runes carved on tree roots as part of a curse. But runes could also be used for healing and protection; an episode in *Egil's Saga* tells how the Icelandic warrior-poet Egil Skallagrimsson carved and blooded runes on a drinking horn filled with poisoned ale, causing the horn to burst and saving Egil from death. Healing talismans have to be used carefully: *Egil's Saga* also tells how a girl became sick when a whale bone with poorly carved runes was placed in her bed. Egil carved new runes and made the girl well. As he said, "No one should write runes who can't read what he carves; a mystery mistaken can bring men to misery."

How do we know what the runes mean?

Several poems have survived from England and Scandinavia that list each rune and give clues to its meaning in a stanza. These include the Old Norwegian Rune Poem, the Old Icelandic Rune Poem, and the Old English Rune Poem. Translations of the rune poems appear at the end of this booklet.

Many clues to the runes' uses and meanings can also be found in the *Poetic Edda*, a collection of Old Norse mythological and heroic poems. Other clues are scattered through the sagas, the prose tales of Iceland that preserve stories and traditions from the Viking Age. Carvings, memorial stones, and other artifacts often yield further clues to how the runes should be used. Finally, the intuition and inspiration of knowledgeable runemasters, guided by the surviving ancient lore and by considerable practical experience, has enabled us to construct an esoteric understanding of the runes.

What is a bindrune?

A bindrune is a symbol made of two or more runes that share strokes. Some bindrunes were used simply to save space, rather like we would use abbreviations in modern English. In other cases, bindrunes were (and are) used magically, to combine the influences of two or more runes. For example, a talisman to gain wealth might include the *fehu* rune on it—but money becomes a source of strife if it's hoarded; it has to circulate freely. Thus if you wanted to attract money but avoid greed and stinginess, you might combine *fehu* with *gebo*. Several amulets have been found that combine *gebo* and *ansuz* in a bindrune. This is an abbreviation for *gibu auja* ("I give good luck"). It also can be read as "gift of a god" or "give inspiration". A spearshaft found at Kragehul, Denmark bears a long inscription that also includes three bindrunes of *gebo* and *ansuz*; in this case, it might be part of an incantation ("*ga ga ga!*") to be shouted as the spear was thrown. More complex bindrunes and rune-like symbols appear in later medieval Icelandic books of magic.

Bindrunes must be made with care. Many runemasters feel that a bindrune that combines poorly matched or conflicting runes may have unexpected effects, or backfire completely.

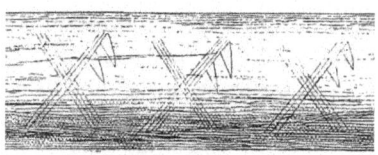
Bindrunes on the Kragehul spearshaft

What is *wyrd*?

Wyrd is a very simple concept that is oddly difficult to translate, but it has to be understood in order to use the runes correctly. Heroic poems such as *Beowulf* often include statements to the effect that "no man may escape his wyrd." The word often is translated as "fate" or "destiny". However, "fate" often implies that something in the future is fixed and can't be altered. Wyrd is a much more dynamic concept than that.

The word "wyrd" was originally a verb tense, meaning "it has become." The word is also related to words meaning "to turn." So wyrd means "what has happened; the way things have turned out." The same word in Norse, *urðr*, is the name of one of the Norns, three powerful beings who shape time. The other two Norns are Verðandi, literally "becoming", and Skuld, "what should be." Urðr, Verðandi and Skuld are not exactly "Past, Present and Future"; Skuld does not represent a fixed future. Instead, Skuld is "what ought to happen; what would be expected to happen"—always subject to change. Heathens saw the past—"what has become"—as constantly guiding and directing the present and the future, but not determining them completely. Wyrd is the force by which the past shapes the future—something like *karma*, but without the moralistic overtones that the concept of *karma* sometimes takes on.

One of the most powerful images in Norse mythology is of the Well of Wyrd; a great seething spring. The Norns sit at the Well, at the foot of the World Tree, which holds all the universes of men, gods and other beings. Past actions drop into the Well of Wyrd, forming layers of *ørlög* ("primal law"). These actions eventually come back into the present, as the Norns take water from the Well to nourish the growth of the Tree.

Another metaphor for wyrd is the weaving of a great tapestry. Countless threads have already gone into the weaving, which have set the pattern of the tapestry. However, a weaver can constantly change the growing pattern as she goes along, depending on her will, her skill, and on what material she has to work with.

It's a little misleading to think of the runes as a tool for "fortune-telling" or "knowing the future"— by definition, you can't know the future, because the future is always in flux. What you can do with runes is investigate past cause and effect. Knowing and meditating on the runes can show you the wyrd that has already been laid down, the threads that have already been woven into the pattern of your life. The runes can help you see how that pattern is affecting your present situation. They can also give you an idea of what is likely to happen if the pattern continues—what the "path of least resistance" is. Experienced runemasters can understand this pattern a little better than most people, and can sometimes use their knowledge to consciously redirect and shape the pattern that wyrd is making. But in the end, you are responsible for setting your own wyrd. You can strive to shape your wyrd for better or worse—but in the end, whatever it brings must be met with courage and dignity. Even our Gods are subject to wyrd.

What is the religious significance of the runes?

In Scandinavian myth, the runes were first grasped by the god Odin, the god of wisdom, death, battle, poetry, and fury (among other things). The myth tells how Odin underwent an ordeal in which he hung from the World Tree for nine nights, pierced by a spear, until he grasped the runes. Odin later gave knowledge of the runes to all beings. The story is told in the Old Norse poem *Hávamál*, one of many poems in the *Poetic Edda*. Another poem in the *Poetic Edda*, known as *Rígspula*, tells how rune knowledge was specifically taught to humans by the god Heimdall. These myths refer not to the origin of the rune letters, but to the grasping of the secret meanings behind them. Runes can be thought of as reflecting parts of the human mind, and also as dynamic forces and patterns of manifestation working throughout all the worlds of the cosmos.

In the *Hávamál*, Odin asks us:

> *Do you know how you must carve? Do you know how you must read?*
> *Do you know how you must color? Do you know how you must test?*

This verse refers both to the making of rune inscriptions, by carving them and by coloring or staining the carvings, and to knowing and interpreting their meanings, both as letters of the alphabet, and as symbols of energy manifestation in all the worlds.

Today, a growing number of people are seriously returning to the ancient myths and practices, reviving the religion of the ancient Germanic peoples. This revived religion is variously known as Ásatrú, Heathenry, the Elder Troth, the Northern Tradition, and other names. Not all followers of this religion (usually known as Heathens or Ásatrúar) practice divination or other forms of magic with the runes, and not all persons interested in the runes identify with this path. Nonetheless, almost all Heathens know something about runes, and honor them as meaningful and sacred symbols. Anyone who wants to understand the runes, whatever his or her spiritual path, needs to learn, understand, and respect the mythology behind them, at the very least. Serious students of the runes should not only memorize the names and sounds of the runes, but should learn to meditate on each rune in order to absorb its meaning into themselves. Runes are not just cool symbols or "secret letters". They are holy, and they should be treated as such.

A GUIDE TO THE RUNES OF THE ELDER FUTHARK

ᚠ **fehu** (cattle)—*f*

The word *fehu* originally meant "cattle", but it later came to mean "money" or "portable wealth"—a holdover from the days when a man's wealth was measured by how many cows he had! *Fehu* can also represent vital energy, or talents and skills (which themselves are a kind of "money in the bank"). The rune poems warn, however, that wealth breeds greed and misery unless it is allowed to circulate. As the Icelandic Rune Poem says, "Wealth causes strife among kinsmen." (Anyone who has ever had to deal with a contested will or a messy divorce will understand this aspect of *fehu* immediately!) The Old English Rune Poem tells us that "every man should deal it our freely": *fehu* causes problems if it stagnates. Finally, *fehu* is associated with fire: a source of warmth, but also a source of destruction if not carefully used.

Cow depicted on the Hunninge picture-stone, Gotland, Sweden

ᚢ **uruz** (wild ox)—long *u* or *oo*; also used for *v*

Variants: ᚣ (Anglo-Saxon futhorc; given the name *yr*, "yew bow", and moved to the end)

The aurochs, or European wild ox, was closely related to domestic cattle, but was a ferocious and untamable animal. Unfortunately, the aurochs is extinct today, but Julius Caesar described them in *The Gallic Wars*: "Great is their strength and great is their speed, and they spare neither man nor beast once sighted." The Old English Rune Poem calls *uruz* "a most dangerous beast fighting with its horns." The Norwegian and Icelandic poems change the name of this rune to *úr*, meaning "slag" and "drizzle," probably because aurochs were extinct in Scandinavia and the original name no longer made sense.

Uruz thus stands for untamed energy, wild and independent. In human affairs it can stand for masculine strength, virility, and courage, and the will to rid oneself of inner obstacles. It can be used to strengthen the will and personality, and to smash down obstacles; it can also be a powerful healing rune. But more negatively, it can manifest in aggression, violence, arrogance, and misapplied force.

*Bronze aurochs.
Viking Age,
Akershus, Norway.*

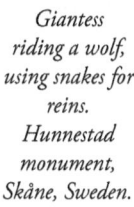 **thurisaz** (giant), or **thorn** (thorn)—*th*

In Heathen mythology, the race of beings called the giants, etins, thurses or jotnar often represent the "blind" forces of nature. This rune stands both for the giants and for the god Thor, the storm-god and lightning-wielder, himself the son of a giantess. Thor constantly battles against the giants—not to wipe them all out, but to maintain the natural balance so that humans can live in the universe. In the Anglo-Saxon Futhorc, this rune was renamed *thorn*: "very sharp for everyone who grabs it." *Thurisaz* can be a powerful rune of defense, but like any weapon, it must be used with caution, or else it can cause chaos and destruction. The Norwegian and Icelandic rune poems call this rune "the sickness of women," and the poem *Skírnismál* in the *Poetic Edda* depicts a man carving this rune to curse a woman.

Giantess riding a wolf, using snakes for reins. Hunnestad monument, Skåne, Sweden.

ᚠ **ansuz** (god, especially Odin)—*a*; in the Anglo-Saxon futhorc the corresponding rune is ᚩ, *óss*, representing short *o*

Alternate forms: ✱ (some Elder Futhark inscriptions)

Variants: ᚪ (*ac*, long *a*) and ᚫ (*æsc*, the sound in "cat") in the Anglo-Saxon Futhorc

The word *ansuz* in Proto-Germanic became *Æsir* in Old Norse. The Æsir are a tribe of gods; their leader is the god Odin (Wotan in German, Woden in Old English). Odin is the winner of all the runes, but he is especially associated with this rune. Among other things, Odin is the giver of inspiration and poetry, but also the giver of fury and rage—his very name means "the furious." For this reason, this rune is associated with inspiration, insight, and higher states of consciousness. A bone amulet dating to 750 AD found in Lindholm, Sweden, has this rune carved eight times in a row, possibly invoking Odin's wisdom. In the Norwegian Rune Poem, this rune's name became *óss*, "estuary", but its description as "the way of most journeys" retains a link with Odin, who is known for traveling the world in many forms.

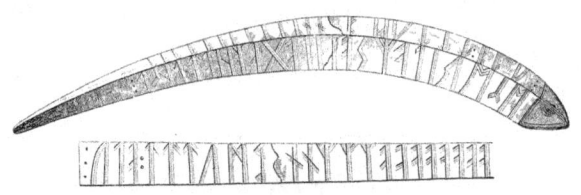

Amulet from Lindholm, Sweden

ᛗ **raidho** (riding)—*r*

The rune poems call *raidho* "the toil of the horse." *Raidho* means journeying and travel, both in space and in time. It can be used to protect travelers. Many modern runecasters see it as a metaphor for the "journey of life," and as the rune of communication. The ancient Scandinavians saw the Sun and Moon as being drawn across the sky in horse-drawn chariots. In ancient Germanic rituals described by the Roman author Tacitus, a statue of the earth goddess Nerthus was drawn in a chariot around the land; a truce was always declared during the time of her procession. Thus *raidho* symbolizes the cyclical rhythms of the natural world and the rituals and days of the human calendar. In this respect *raidho* is similar to *jera*. Finally, like *tiwaz*, *raidho* is connected with right action, right behavior, law, and integration of individuals into communities—the results of living in harmony with natural laws and cycles. Modern Heathens often associate it with the god of justice and judgment, Forseti.

Bronze Age solar chariot, Trundholm, Denmark

< **kenaz** (torch) or **kaunaz** (sore)—*k*; in Old English it came to represent a *ch* sound

Alternate forms: ᚴ (Younger Futhark), ᚳ (Anglo-Saxon Futhorc)

Variants: ᚴ (Younger Futhark; a "dotted" form of the *k* rune was sometimes used for *g*)

A torch is a way of harnessing fire for human benefit. *Kenaz* is associated with creativity, exploration, knowledge, and craftsmanship; it takes the fire of *fehu* and applies it for a purpose. At best, this is a constructive act. At worst, the alternative name *kaunaz* (sore) for this rune, found in some of the poems, reminds us that creative energy can be misapplied—gaining knowledge is not always comfortable. The Norse poem *Hávamál* describes good conversation as being like a flame passed from one torch to another, until all are ablaze and the room is filled with light. Thus *kenaz* is a rune of higher mental activity. Some also see *kenaz* as connected with death, initiation and rebirth—the purifying flames of the forge, or the flames of the pyre that free the soul.

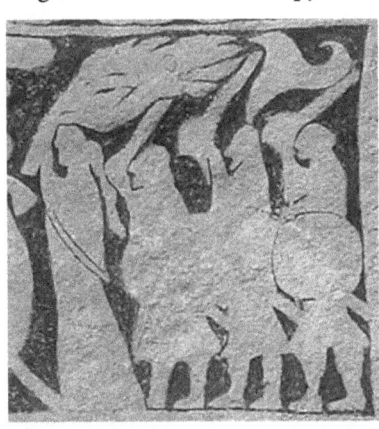

Torchbearing woman leading warriors. Stora Hammars I stone, Gotland, Sweden.

X **gebo** (gift)—hard *g*

Variants: ᚷ (Anglo-Saxon Futhorc rune *gar*, used for hard *g*)

Generosity was one of the highest virtues in ancient Germanic societies. Gifts exchanged between friends bound the friendship more closely, as long as the gifting was equal ad reciprocal—the *Hávamál* says that friends should always gladden each other with the exchange of gifts, and also that "a gift always looks for repayment." Gifts from a ruler to his people kept them loyal and faithful; in poetry, "ring-giver" and "gold-friend" were some of the highest compliments that could be paid to a ruler. A stingy ruler was despised. *Gebo* is a rune of equal exchange, alliances, friendship and hospitality, but it also means obligation. It keeps the power of *fehu* from stagnating and becoming destructive. It may also be used in love magic to bring about a stable and fulfilling partnership, as long as balance is kept.

Viking Age gold arm-ring, Stockholm, Sweden

ᚹ **wunjo** (joy)—*w*

Wunjo is exactly what it says: the rune of joy and cheerfulness. Not simply an outward show of happiness; *wunjo* is an inner resource that can carry the one who has it through difficult times. As the hero Sigurd says, "To be glad is better than of gloomy mood, whether all fall fair or foul." *Wunjo* means perseverance and strength of will, and the willingness to meet challenges cheerfully rather than giving in to despair. It can be used to ward off depression and bring emotional and physical healing. It is also a rune of friendship and kinfolk—"man is cheered by man," as the *Hávamál* says. In the same poem, Odin tells of a rune spell that he knows: "where hatred grows among princes, I can quickly settle it." This shows the power of *wunjo* for good. Some modern writers link the shape of this rune letter with a banner—that is, with something to rally around.

Raven Banner at the Battle of Hastings, 1066 CE, as depicted on the Bayeux Tapestry.

ᚺ hagalaz (hail)—*h*

Alternate form: ᛡ (Younger Futhark), ᚻ (Anglo-Saxon Futhorc)

Anyone who has been through a major hailstorm knows that hail is a destructive and damaging force. Yet this rune isn't wholly negative. The poems all describe *hagalaz* as "white grain"—and by definition, grain is a seed. The Old English poem describes how hail eventually melts and turns to water, which nourishes new growth; the Norse poems call hail "the sickness of snakes"—something that does harm to dangerous reptiles. Thus *hagalaz* can mean the destruction of old patterns, but it ultimately can clear the way for the creation of something new and better. Despite its association with calamity, several modern runemasters see *hagalaz* as representing the "seed crystal" from which the entire universe came into existence. It might not be inappropriate to call this the "Big Bang" rune.

Hailstones.

ᚾ **naudhiz** (need)—*n*
Alternate form: ᚾ (Younger Futhark)

The rune poems call *naudhiz* "troublesome work" and "a difficult situation," and the Norwegian Rune Poem associates the line "the naked freeze in the frost" with this rune. *Naudhiz* is associated with hardship, poverty, isolation, and stress. However, the Old English Rune Poem tells us that *naudhiz* can be "help and healing, if they heed it sooner." *Naudhiz* is connected with "need-fire", fire made by rubbing sticks together. It's very difficult to make a fire that way, but it may be necessary to keep from freezing to death—and need-fire was considered holy by the heathen Germans. In Old Norse, *nauðr*, "need," could also mean "childbirth; labor." In all of these meanings, *naudhiz* represents a struggle or difficulty—that nonetheless may leave a person stronger and better for having undergone it. The saying "That which does not kill me makes me stronger" applies to this rune!

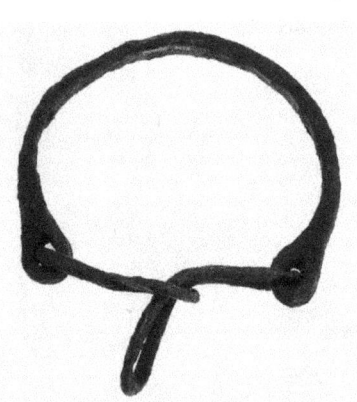

Viking-era iron neck shackle, probably used on slaves. Birka, Uppland, Sweden.

isa (ice)—*i or ee*

The Norse myths tell how the universe came into being from fire and ice—or, as physicists might call them now, energy and matter. *Isa* represents stability, permanence, and peace; it's the exact opposite of the fiery rune *fehu*. On the other hand, it can also represent stagnation and constraint. In human affairs, it can mean calmness, patience, concentration, the ego ("I"), and the numbing of pain. More negatively, it can stand for inertia and sloth. Ice can be beautiful—the Old English Poem states that "a floor wrought of frost is a fair sight." Yet ice can't be trusted; other rune poems call *isa* "exceedingly slippery," and the *Hávamál* warns against trusting thin ice: "praise ice when you've crossed it." We still refer to a perilous situation as "skating on thin ice." Thus *isa* can indicate hidden dangers or warn of a false sense of security.

Metapodial (lower leg) bone of a cow, shaped and polished for use as an ice skate, as was typical in the Viking Age. The skate is pictured upside down, with the gliding surface on top. Birka, Uppland, Sweden.

⟨ **jera** (year, harvest)—consonantal *y*
Alternate form: ϕ (Anglo-Saxon Futhorc); ↑, ↥ (Younger Futhark, called *ár* and used for long *a*)

Jera stands for the cycle of the seasons and the agricultural year; the Icelandic Rune Poem calls it "a good summer and a ripened field." It resolves the opposed forces of fire and ice so that they complement each other for the benefit of everyone. *Jera* is a rune of natural growth, patience, long-term planning, hard work slowly coming to fruition, and awareness of the changing seasons. Heathens often associate it, as well as *ingwaz*, with the god Freyr, whom the Norse prayed to for "peace and good seasons." In divination, *jera* can mean that the results of past actions are being "harvested"—hopefully for the better, but as the Icelandic *Njál's Saga* warns us, "When ill seed has been sown, so an ill crop will spring from it." The more modern saying "What comes around, goes around" is appropriate to this rune.

Runestone, Stentoften, Sweden. The middle vertical line reads **hathuwolafr gaf j**, *"Hathuwolaf gave* jera*"—a king gave peace and good seasons to his people.*

ᛇ **eiwaz** (yew tree)—a vowel often transliterated *ï*; may be used today for short *i*

Heathens see the universe as being supported by a great tree called Yggdrasill, the center and axis of all that is. This rune is a symbol of that tree, which is sometimes identified as a yew. *Eiwaz*, at the center of the futhark, is the stable point around which the cycles of the world revolve (*jera*). Yews are powerful in folklore, and rune amulets found at Britsum, Arum and Westeremden in Frisia were carved from yew. Yews are evergreen, alive when all other trees have died, but also highly poisonous. They are traditionally planted in graveyards in northern Europe. Thus this rune, rarely used in writing, is the rune of life and death and rebirth, and of the synthesis between opposing forces. Finally, yew was the favored wood for making bows, and is associated with Ullr, the god of hunting and archery who protects fighters. This rune can be a protective symbol; the Old English rune *yr*, which means "yew bow" and may share some of this rune's meaning, is called "a piece of wargear" in the Old English Rune Poem.

European yew, Taxus baccata

ᛈ **perthro** (dice-cup or gambling game)—*p*

This rune was not often used in early inscriptions; its sound seems to have been rare in Germanic languages at the time. The meaning of the word *perthro* isn't clear, but the likeliest idea is that it has something to do with gaming, possibly meaning a board-game piece or a dice-cup. The Old English Rune Poem calls this rune "play and laughter for noble men, where warriors sit in the beer-hall, happy together." Tacitus reports that the Germanic tribes of his time (ca. 100 CE) were immensely fond of gambling, sometimes even wagering their own freedom. Yet *perthro* isn't purely a rune of amusement. Gambling and board games are linked in the heathen lore with *wyrd*, a concept something like "fate" but less rigid. Many runecasters today see *perthro* as the "Mother-Rune," the rune of wyrd itself. It is the Mystery from which all the runes spring, and symbolizes the Well of Wyrd. *Perthro* is also connected with birth. Several modern rune experts have found that *perthro* in a divination means that an outcome is still "up in the air", not yet fixed—or, perhaps, that the questioner is not supposed to know the answer.

Viking Era dice. Oslo, Norway.

ᛉ **elhaz** (elk)—originally *z*; in Norse a sound between *zh* and *r* at the end of words; *x* in Old English

Variant forms: ᛦ (Younger Futhark, moved to the end and renamed *yr*, "yew")

Elhaz means "elk", but is also linked to the old Germanic word *algiz,* meaning "protection" or "sanctuary." The old custom of putting elk horns on the roofs of houses shows the link between these meanings: this is a rune of protection and defense. In the Old English Rune Poem, it is identified as a sedge, a grass with sharp-edged, swordlike leaves that cut anyone who tries to pull them up. It also is a rune of hallowing sacred space, and of connection with higher powers: *elhaz* shows the posture that a worshipper stands in when calling upon the Gods, proudly standing straight (not kneeling or bowing!) with arms raised. In personal development, this rune can be used to rid oneself of guilt and self-condemnation. One of the most powerful protective bindrunes, the *aegishjalmar* or "Helm of Awe", consists of eight *elhaz*-runes radiating from a common point.

Stone Age rock art showing elk. Moelv, Norway.

ᚺ **sowilo** (sun)—*s*

Alternate forms: ᛊ (Elder Futhark), ᛋ (Younger Futhark)

Like its neighboring rune *tiwaz*, *sowilo* is a rune of victory. In northern Europe, the sun rises late and sets early all through the winter; in the far north it may not rise at all. The return of the sun's warmth and light is a victory of light over darkness, and a cause for celebration. This is reflected in the rune poems; the *s*-rune is "the lands' ray of light" in the Norwegian Rune Poem, "shining glory and ice's sorrow" in the Icelandic Rune Poem, "ever a joy in the hopes of seafarers" in the Old English Rune Poem. *Sowilo* is linked, in modern thought, with healing and with restoring life energy, and with personal power and the will to act. In magic it can be used to aid a good cause to triumph (although if the cause isn't truly good, the magic may easily backfire). Finally, it is a rune of honor; a verse in the *Hávamál* links the light of the sun with a life lived without disgrace.

Sun motif from the Havor picture stone, Gotland, Sweden.

↑ **tiwaz** (the god Tyr)—*t*
Alternate forms: ↑ (Younger Futhark)

The god Tyr or Tiw is the god of rightness and cosmic order; the Norse knew him to be both wise and brave. His rune is a rune of victory; the Norse poem *Sigrdrífumál* recommends that a warrior who wants victory should carve runes on his sword and call on Tyr. This rune is also linked with the Old English word *tir*, meaning "glory." But Tyr is also the god who sacrificed his hand, so that the wolf Fenrir—the embodiment of the forces of chaos and destruction—could be bound before he could destroy the cosmos. The "Icelandic Rune Poem" calls Tyr "one-handed god, leavings of the wolf." *Tiwaz* can thus mean a sacrifice to gain a greater good: "victory doesn't come for free." The Old English Rune Poem calls this rune a star that "keeps faith well with nobles; over the mists of night it never fails." Thus *tiwaz* is also a rune of high ideals, faithfulness, loyalty, guidance, and trust in one's self.

Tyr (Tiw) setting his hand in the mouth of Fenrir. Sockburn, UK.

ᛒ berkano (birch tree)—*b*

In northern Europe, birch trees are the first to leaf out as winter is ending. The rune poems call the birch "leafy twig," "laden with leaves," "the greenest-leaved limbs," associating it with the return of spring and with new life and growth. In contemporary Heathen thought, *berkano* can represent renewal, but also concealment: the slow, hidden growth of potential until it is the right time for it to come forth. We also associate this rune with the goddesses of the Norse tradition, especially Frigga and Freya. On another level, it is a rune of female fertility and women's mysteries. Along with *perthro*, it is one of the "birth-runes" that aid in pregnancy and childbirth; the poem *Sigrdrífumál* tells us that certain runes may be drawn on the palms of midwives to help them assist women in delivery.

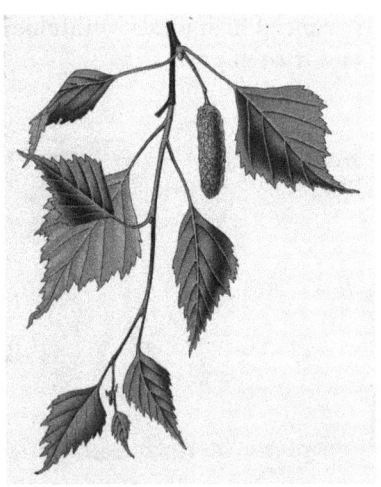

European silver birch, Betula pendula.

ᛖ ehwaz (horse)—*e*

Think of the close bond between an experienced rider and his or her horse; the two communicate almost telepathically. This rune is a rune of trust, and of close emotional and spiritual bonds. The Old English Rune Poem states that *ehwaz* "for the restless is ever a help." Like *raidho*, *ehwaz* can indicate a journey, whether outward or inward. It can also symbolize the integration of the various parts of the psyche into a harmonious whole. Norse mythology describes many of the gods as riding horses; modern Heathens consider the horse to be especially sacred to the gods Odin and Freyr. According to Tacitus, some Germanic tribes observed the actions of sacred horses to divine the will of the Gods; thus this rune, along with *elhaz*, can be a rune of receiving divine wisdom.

Design on the Möjebro stone, Sweden. The runes read from bottom to top and right to left: **frawaradaR ana haha islaginaR**, *meaning uncertain but possibly "Frawaradar was slain on his horse."*

ᛗ **mannaz** (man, human being)—*m*
Alternate forms: ᛦ, ᛧ, ᛁ (Younger Futhark)

Mannaz—"man" in the sense of "human being", not limited to males—is linked with the god Heimdall, the guardian of the gods' realm, Ásgarðr. The poem *Rígsþula* tells how he fathered the different classes of humans and taught runes to his descendants. The Norwegian and Icelandic rune poems state that "Man is the increase of earth"—we grow from the soil that we depend on for food—and the Old English poem reminds us that our "frail flesh" must return to the earth. We are destined to die and return to the earth—but we still carry Heimdall's gift, the spark of divine heritage. The *Abecedarium Nordmannicum* calls this rune "man in the middle"—standing in Midgard or "Middle-Earth", between the upper and the lower realms, partaking in the nature of both. *Mannaz* is the rune of the "human condition." Many modern runemasters feel that it stands for the balance of reason and intuition, of mind, soul and spirit. Like *othala*, it may also symbolize inheritance, or wisdom gained from your ancestors.

Human couple on a sheet gold plaque (guldgubber)*, Norway.*

ᛚ **laguz** (lake) or **laukaz** (leek)—*l*

The Vikings and their kin depended on water voyages for their survival and prosperity, but they knew the dangers well. The Old English Rune Poem associates this rune with a stormy sea voyage: "the sea-waves are most terrifying and the sea-stallion [ship] does not obey the bridle." *Laguz* thus has two sides; it can bring benefits or dangers. It may well be one of the "sea-runes" referred to in the poem *Sigrdrífumál* which should be carved on a ship to protect it at sea. In a more psychological sense, *laguz* represents the "deep waters" of the unconscious mind, which can be a source of life-giving insight, but which may also storm and rage, or stagnate and become toxic if not allowed to flow. *Laguz* is also the water within the Well of Wyrd itself, which conceals both great power and potential dangers. This rune's alternative name, *laukaz*, means "leek" or "garlic". Leeks were used in Norse magic to defend against poison.

View of a lake, Store Mosse National Park, Sweden.

◇ **ingwaz** or **ingunaz** (the god Ing)—the **ng** sound, as in **finger** and **ring**
Alternate form: ᛝ (Anglo-Saxon Futhorc)

Ing, or Yngvi as he was called in Sweden, is more commonly known by his title Freyr (in Norse) or Frea (in Old English). Both titles mean "lord," and in some ways Freyr is like the "Lord" of Wiccan tradition. The Norse *Ynglinga saga* tells that Freyr was invoked *til árs ok friðar*, "for peace and good seasons," and called *veraldar goð*, "god of the world" or "god of man's life." Yngvi-Freyr bestows riches, fertility, and other bounty for humans to enjoy. Yet Freyr can be a warrior as well, and he is an ancestor of the old royal families of England and Scandinavia. The *ingwaz* rune is connected with men's lives, including but not limited to sexuality and fertility. Modern runemasters often see it as the male counterpart to *berkano*.

Viking Age statuette identified as the god Freyr. Rällinge, Södermanland, Sweden.

ᛞ **dagaz** (day)—**d**, sometimes **dh** or voiced **th**

In the heroic poems of the Volsung cycle, the heroine Brynhild speaks a prayer after Sigurd has awakened her from a magical sleep: "Hail, ye Day! Hail, ye Day's sons! Hail Night and daughter of Night!" *Dagaz* is the rune of awakening, of enlightenment—of things that "finally dawn on you." *Dagaz* can stand for the resolution of paradoxes, and for full awareness of one's surroundings. It is a rune of revelation, unlike *perthro*, which is a rune of concealment and mystery. It can mean a new beginning on a higher level, or new insight and wisdom. Finally, in folklore, daylight causes trolls and other night creatures to turn to stone. This rune can be used to protect against literal or figurative "creatures of the night."

Bronze Age rock art showing a probable solar disc. Tanum, Bohuslän, Sweden.

ᛟ **othala** (inheritance)—long *o*

In contrast to *fehu*, which represents "liquid assets" such as money, *othala* is an old term for ancestral land. "Odal-land" was land that had stayed in a family for many generations; the family retained certain legal rights even if they had to sell it. Runestones were often raised on odal-land to record the family's genealogy, tied to its ownership of land. Today, we often see *othala* as a symbol for everything that a person inherits from his or her ancestors. These may include inborn talents, genetic traits, and customs and attitudes learned in the family, as well as physical property. *Othala* is also a rune of the family itself, of ancestors and kinfolk, whether by blood or by adoption. It symbolizes boundaries and stability.

Gold ring from Pietroassa, Romania, made by the Goths, probably in the late 300s CE. The runes read **gutaniowihailag**, *which may mean "The Goths' othala [ancestral property], sacred, holy."*

THE RUNE POEMS

Norwegian Rune Poem

ᚠ **Wealth** causes kin-strife;
    a wolf grows up in the forest.
ᚢ **Slag** comes from bad iron;
    reindeer often run on hard snow.
ᚦ **Giant** causes sickness for women;
    few are cheered by evil.
ᚬ **River-mouth** is the course of most journeys;
    but a sheath is the course for swords.
ᚱ **Riding**, they say, is worst for horses.
    Regin forged the best sword.[1]
ᚴ **Sore** is trouble for children;
    pain makes a man pale.
ᚼ **Hail** is coldest grain;
    Christ shaped the world in olden times.
ᚾ **Need** gives few choices;
    a naked man freezes in frost.
ᛁ **Ice** we call a broad bridge;
    a blind man needs to be led.
ᛅ **Harvest** is good for men;
    I suppose that Frodi[2] was generous.
ᛋ **Sun** is the lands' ray of light;
    I bow to holy judgment.
ᛏ **Tyr** is the one-handed god;
    a smith must often blow the bellows.

---

1. Regin reforged Gram, the sword of the hero Sigurd, in *Völsunga saga*.
2. A legendary king whose reign was famous for prosperity and peace.

ᛒ **Birch** has limbs with greenest limbs;
   Loki was lucky in his deceit.
ᛘ **Man** is the increase of earth;
   great is the grip of a hawk.
ᛚ **Lake** is a waterfall plunging
   from a mountain; gold rings are treasures.
ᛦ **Yew** is the greenest tree in winter;
   when it burns, it often singes.

Icelandic Rune Poem

ᚠ **Wealth** is kin-strife   and household's joy
   and serpents' path.
ᚢ **Drizzle** is clouds' weeping   and hay-destroyer
   and herdsman's hate.
ᚦ **Giant** is women's pain   and cliff-dweller
   and Valruna's husband.
ᚬ **God of the Æsir** is Gaut[3] the ancient   and
   Asgard's chieftain
   and Valhall's ruler.
ᚱ **Riding** is joy for the rider   and swift travel
   and horse's labor.
ᚴ **Sore** is children's pain   and a struggle
   and home of gangrene.
ᚼ **Hail** is cold grain   and a lump-shower
   and snakes' sickness.
ᚾ **Need** is the slave's struggle   and a stark choice
   and cold, wet work.
ᛁ **Ice** is rivers' bark   and waves' thatch
   and danger to doomed men.

---

3. A by-name for the god Odin.

ᛇ **Harvest** is a boon to men   and a good summer
      and full-grown fields.
ᛋ **Sun** is sky's shield   and shining glory
      and ice's sorrow.
ᛏ **Tyr** is a one-handed god   and leavings of the wolf[4]
      and ruler of temples.
ᛒ **Birch** is a leafy limb   and a little tree
      and a glorious growth.
ᛘ **Man** is man's joy   and increase of earth
      and adornment of ships.
ᛚ **Lake** is a welling river   and a wide kettle
      and the fishes' land.
ᛦ **Yew** is a bent bow   and a battle advantage
      and an arrow-launcher.

Old English Rune Poem

ᚠ **Wealth** is consolation to every man.
Every man must   deal it out lavishly
if he wishes to share   in glory before the lord.

ᚢ **Aurochs** is fierce   and hugely horned,
a most dangerous beast   fighting with its horns,
great moor-walker;   it is a bold creature.

ᚦ **Thorn** is sorely sharp;   receiving it is bad
for every warrior,   uncommonly harsh
for every man   that lies among them.

---

4. Refers to the myth of Tyr placing his hand in the mouth of the wolf Fenrir, so that the wolf might be bound.

ᚩ **The Æsir-God** is origin   of all speech,
wisdom's support   and wise men's comfort,
for every prince   prosperity and hope.

ᚱ **Riding** seems easy   inside the home
of every man—but strenuous   for him who sits
on a mighty horse   for miles on the road.

ᚳ **Torch** to every being   is known by its fire,
shining brightly;   it burns most often
where noblemen   are resting inside.

ᚷ **Gifting** is an ornament   and praise to men,
comfort and honor,   and for every wretch
deprived of all else,   it is gain and support.

ᚹ **Joy** belongs to him   who knows few woes,
pains and sorrow,   and himself has
prosperity and bliss   and estate enough.

ᚻ **Hail** is whitest grain;   it whirls from lofty heaven,
windy showers toss it,   then it turns to water.

ᚾ **Need** tightens in the chest,   but often for men's sons
it turns to help and healing,   if they heed it sooner.

ᛁ **Ice** is too cold,   exceedingly slippery;
it glitters, glass-clear,   like gems most of all,
a floor wrought of frost,   fair to the sight.

ᚻ **Harvest** is hope   for humans, when God,
holy king of heaven,   bestows on earth
shining shoots   for rich and for poor.

ᛇ **Yew** on the outside   is not a smooth tree:
firm in the earth,   flame's hard keeper,
underpinned by its roots,   the pride of the estate.

ᛈ **Gambling** is always   play and laughter
for noble men,   where warriors sit
in the beer-hall,   happy together.

ᛉ **Sedge** most often   makes its home in the marsh,
it grows in water,   severely wounds
and burns with blood   every bold man
who makes any   attempt to grasp it.

ᛋ **Sun** is always   seafarers' hope
when it carries them   over the fishes' bath,
and brings to land   the sea-stallion.

ᛏ **Glory / Tyr** is a sign,   it holds well the trust
of noble men,   ever on course,
over night's mists   it never fails.

ᛒ **Birch** bears no fruit—   even so, it bears
shoots with no seeds;   it is splendid in its branches,
high in its crown,   adorned fairly,
laden with leaves, it touches the sky.

ᛖ **Horse** is a joy   for earls among noblemen,
a hoof-proud steed,   whenever heroes,
rich men riding,   bandy words about him—
and for the restless   is ever a comfort.

ᛗ **Man** is dear   to his kinsman, in joy;
yet each is destined   to betray the other,
for by his own judgment   the lord wills
to commit to earth   the wretched flesh.

ᛚ **Lake** is thought   lengthy by people
if they must dare to travel   on a rocking boat,
and the sea-waves   are most terrifying
and the sea-stallion   does not obey the bridle.

ᛝ **Ing** was first   seen by men
among the East-Danes,   until he returned
back over the path;   the wagon followed.
Thus did the Heardings   name the hero.

ᛟ **Estate** is most dear   to every man
if he may always   enjoy prosperity
there in his home   as is right and seemly.

ᛞ **Day** is the lord's message,   dear to men,
the ruler's great light,   happiness and hope
for the use of all,   wealthy and wretched.

ᚪ **Oak** on earth   is fodder for swine,
flesh for men's sons,   and frequently fares

over gannet's bath;   the sea finds out
whether oak   keeps noble trust.

ᚫ **Ash** is most tall,   prized by men,
stiff in its trunk,   holds its place rightly,
though it must fight   against many men.

ᚣ **Yew-bow** is for every   earl and nobleman
a joy and an honor;   it is lovely on a horse,
resolute on a journey,   a piece of battle-gear.

ᛡ **Serpent** is a river-fish,   though it always enjoys
feeding on land;   it has a fine home
surrounded by water,   where it lives happily.

ᛠ **Grave** is terror   to every man,
when swiftly   the flesh, the corpse,
begins to cool,   the pale body to choose
earth for its bed.   Flourishing fails,
joy departs,   manhood ends.

Abecedarium Nordmannicum

ᚠ **Wealth** first, ᚢ **Aurochs** after,
ᚦ **Giant** the third letter,
the ᚭ **Æsir-God** is above him,
write ᚱ **Ride** at the end, ᚴ **Torch** comes next.
ᚼ **Hail**, ᚾ **Need** has
ᛁ **Ice**, ᛅ **Harvest**, ᛋ **Sun**,
ᛏ **Tyr**, ᛒ **Birch**, and ᛘ **Man** in the middle,
ᛚ **Lake** the bright, ᛦ **Yew** holds all.

SOURCES: The oldest known manuscript of the *Norwegian Rune Poem* was found in an old legal manuscript in the Copenhagen University Library. This was lost in a fire in 1728, but not before several copies had been made. My translation is based on the text as restored by Kålund.

There are several manuscripts of the *Icelandic Rune Poem*, which do not agree with each other on all points. I have followed the consensus version published by Page; when this was incomplete, I have usually followed the mansucript AM 687a (Page's manuscript A). I have not included the Latin words and kingly titles attached to each verse.

The *Anglo-Saxon Poem* is known from one manuscript that was destroyed by fire in 1731; fortunately, it had been published in print in 1705. I have translated it from Dobbie's edition.

The *Abecedarium Nordmannicum* is a brief mnemonic poem for the Younger Futhark, written in a mix of Old High German and Old Saxon. I have used the text as published by Dickins.

Dickins, Bruce. *Runic and Heroic Poems of the Old Teutonic Peoples*. Cambridge: Cambridge University Press, 1915.

Dobbie, Elliott Van Kirk. *The Anglo-Saxon Poetic Records. Volume VI: The Anglo-Saxon Minor Poems.* New York: Columbia University Press, 1942.

Kålund, Kristian. "Et Gammel-Norsk Rune-rim og Nogle Islandske Rune-remser." *Småstykker* 1-16, Samfund til Udgivelse af Gammel Nordisk Litteratur. Copenhagen: S. L. Møller, 1884-1891. Pp. 1-21.

Kålund, Kristian, and Sophus Bugge. "Tillæg til *Småstykker* no. 1." *Småstykker* 1-16, Samfund til Udgivelse af Gammel Nordisk Litteratur. Copenhagen: S. L. Møller, 1884-1891. Pp. 100-113.

Page, R. I. *The Icelandic Rune Poem*. London: Viking Society for Northern Research, 1999.

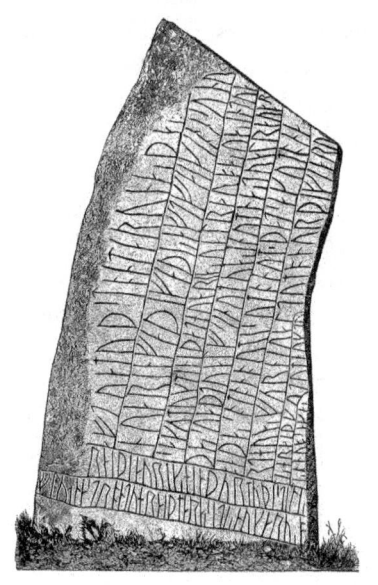

The Rök runestone, Östergötland, Sweden.

How can I find out more about the runes?

There are many books on the runes. Some are well-researched, while others contain flawed information—be careful! Look for books that contain documented references to known texts and artifacts.

Some of the original source texts with the best information on how runes were used in ancient times include:

> Hollander, Lee M. (transl.) *The Poetic Edda.* Austin: University of Texas Press, 1962. Many other translations are available.
>
> Scudder, Bertrand (transl.) *Egil's Saga.* London: Penguin, 2005.
>
> —. *Grettir's Saga.* London Penguin, 2005.
>
> Tacitus (J. B. Rives, transl.) *The Agricola and the Germania.* London: Penguin, 2010.
>
> Waggoner, Ben (transl.) *The Hávamál.* The Troth, 2017.

For historical overviews of the runes, the following books are excellent:

> Elliot, R.W.V. *Runes: An Introduction.* 2nd ed. Manchester: Manchester University Press, 1987.
>
> Findell, Martin. *Runes.* London: British Museum Pres, 2014.
>
> MacLeod, Mindy, and Bernard Mees. *Runic Amulets and Magic Objects.* Woodbridge: Boydell, 2006.
>
> Page, R. I. *Reading the Past: Runes.* Berkeley: University of California Press, 1987.

Pollington, Stephen. *Rudiments of Runelore.* 3rd edition. Hockwold-cum-Wilton: Anglo-Saxon Books, 1995.

To learn more about the magical and religious meanings of the runes, we recommend these books:
Gerard, Katie. *Odin's Gateways.* London: Avalonia, 2011.
Gundarsson, Kveldulf. *The Teutonic Way.* Saga Press, 2018.
Paxson, Diana. *Taking Up the Runes.* York Beach: Weiser, 2005.
Sheffield, Ann Gróa. *Long Branches: Runes of the Younger Futhark.* Lulu, 2013.

For more information on the revitalized religion of Heathenry or Ásatrú, we recommend these books:
Members of the Troth. *Our Troth.* 2 vols. CreateSpace, 2005-2006.
Paxson, Diana. *Essential Ásatrú.* Citadel, 2008.
Lafayllve, Patricia. *A Practical Heathen's Guide to Ásatrú.* Llewellyn, 2013.

What is The Troth?

The Troth is a religious organization, dedicated to exploring, practicing and promoting the pre-Christian religion of the Germanic-speaking peoples of England, Scandinavia, Germany, and surrounding regions. Our religion today includes various traditions and names: Ásatrú, Heathenry, the Elder Troth, Northern Tradition, Forn Sed, Fyrn Sidu, Urglaawe, and others. Although there are many variations in beliefs and practices within this faith, we all share a defining personal loyalty to, or "Troth" with, the gods and goddesses of the Northlands, such as Odin, Thor, Frigga, and many others; a deep respect for our Germanic religious, cultural and historical heritage; and a strong determination to practice the moral principles followed by our noble predecessors.

The Troth publishes a quarterly magazine, *Idunna*, along with other writings on heathen belief and practice. We serve as a networking organization for individuals and kindreds, and we try to assist our members to form local groups to practice our religion and make it more widely available. Once a year, the Troth sponsors a major gathering, Trothmoot, at which members and interested folks conduct workshops and ceremonies, and discuss and demonstrate their many skills and practices. The Troth also operates a clergy training program, incorporating both academic study of lore and theology and training in ceremonial practice, group organization, and counseling. We are incorporated as a non-profit religious corporation in the state of Texas, and are recognized by the U.S. Internal Revenue Service as a tax-exempt religious organization.

The Troth believes that the Gods call whom they will—regardless of race, ethnic origin, gender, or sexual orientation. To hear their call is a joy, an honor, and also a duty. If you hear that call, and if you are willing to live by our values and honor our Gods, then we invite you to take your place among friends and kin, and bring new honor and strength to our ancient Heathen faith.

How can I find out more about The Troth?
- Visit the main website of The Troth at **http://www.thetroth.org/**
- The Troth has a network of local coordinators, or "Stewards", who are happy to answer questions and provide contacts. To find your nearest Steward, go to **https://thetroth.org/programs/steward/map.html**
- E-mail the Troth at **troth-contact@thetroth.org**
- Write to the Troth at the address on the first page of this booklet.

ILLUSTRATION CREDITS

Cover, above: Bracteate (stamped gold medallion), Vadstena, Sweden. The runes read counterclockwise from the top: **luwatuwa** (probably a magic formula) and then the complete Elder Futhark. Swedish Historical Museum, object 110733. CC BY 2.5.

Cover, below: Runestone fragment from Birka, Sweden; the runes read **. . . stain+rais. . .**, "Steinn raised" [this stone]. Swedish Historical Museum, object 1089318. CC BY 2.5.

Kylver futhark: Agrell, Sigurd. *Lapptrummor och Runmagi*. Lund: Gleerup, 1934. Public domain.

Kragehul spearshaft: Stephens, George. *Handbook of the Old Northern Runic Monuments of Scandinavia and England*. London: Williams and Norgate, 1884. Public Domain.

Fehu: Gotland Museum. Public Domain.

Uruz: Kulturhistorisk Museum, University of Oslo, Norway. CC BY-SA 4.0.

Thurisaz: Photo by Hedning, Wikimedia Commons, CC SA 3.0.

Ansuz: Stephens, George. *Handbook of the Old Northern Runic Monuments of Scandinavia and England*. London: Williams and Norgate, 1884. Public Domain.

Raidho: National Museum of Denmark. CC BY-SA 2.0.

Kenaz: Swedish Historical Museum, object 108206. CC BY 2.5.

Gebo: Swedish Historical Museum, object 110025. CC BY 2.5.

Wunjo: Wikimedia Commons. Public Domain.

Hagalaz: Photo by Richard Wheeler, Wikimedia Commons, CC SA 3.0.

Naudhiz: Swedish Historical Museum, object 608426. CC BY 2.5.

Isa: Swedish Historical Museum, object 987944. CC BY 2.5.

Jera: Stephens, George. *Handbook of the Old Northern Runic Monuments of Scandinavia and England.* London: Williams and Norgate, 1884. Public Domain.

Eiwaz: Thomé, Otto Wilhelm. *Flora von Deutschland, Österreich, und Schweiz.* 4 vols. Gera: Friedrich von Zezschwitz, 1903–1905. Public Domain.

Perthro: Kulturhistorisk Museum, University of Oslo, Norway. CC BY-SA 4.0.

Elhaz: Photo by Lexidh, Wikimedia Commons. Rights granted.

Sowilo: Swedish Historical Museum, object 108201. CC BY 2.5.

Tiwaz: Knowles, W. H. "Sockburn Church." *Transactions of the Architectural and Archaeological Society of Durham and Northumberland,* vol. 5 (1907), pp. 99-120. Public Domain.

Berkano: Thomé, Otto Wilhelm. *Flora von Deutschland, Österreich, und Schweiz.* 4 vols. Gera: Friedrich von Zezschwitz, 1903–1905. Public Domain.

Ehwaz: Stephens, George. *Handbook of the Old Northern Runic Monuments of Scandinavia and England.* London: Williams and Norgate, 1884. Public Domain.

Mannaz: Kulturhistorisk Museum, University of Oslo, Norway. CC BY-SA 4.0.

Laguz: Photo by Boatbuilder, Wikimedia Commons, CC SA 3.0.

Ingwaz: Swedish Historical Museum, object 109037. CC BY 2.5.

Dagaz: Swedish National Antiquities Board / Riksantikvarieämbetet. CC BY 2.5.

Othala: Stephens, George. *Handbook of the Old Northern Runic Monuments of Scandinavia and England.* London: Williams and Norgate, 1884. Public Domain.

Rök stone and bracteates: Stephens, George. *Handbook of the Old Northern Runic Monuments of Scandinavia and England.* London: Williams and Norgate, 1884. Public Domain.

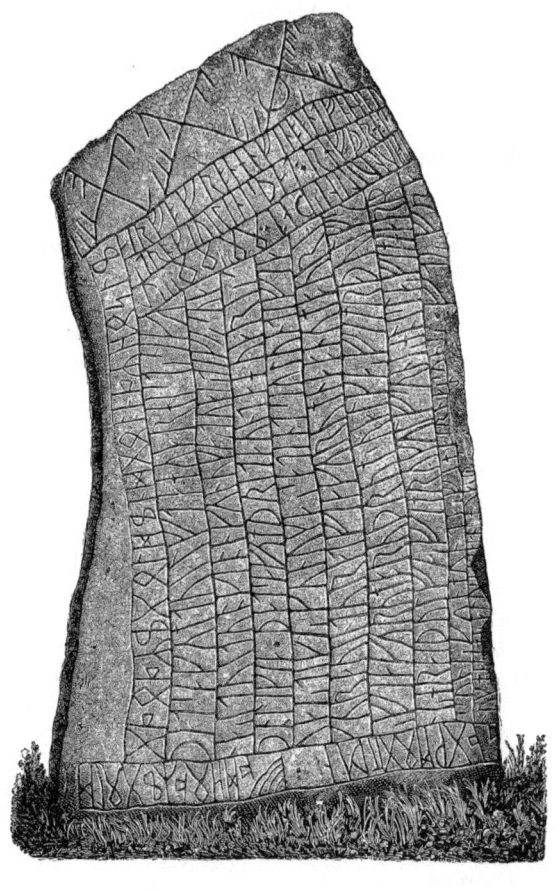

The Rök runestone, Östergötland, Sweden.
This side shows encoded runes along the top of the stone.

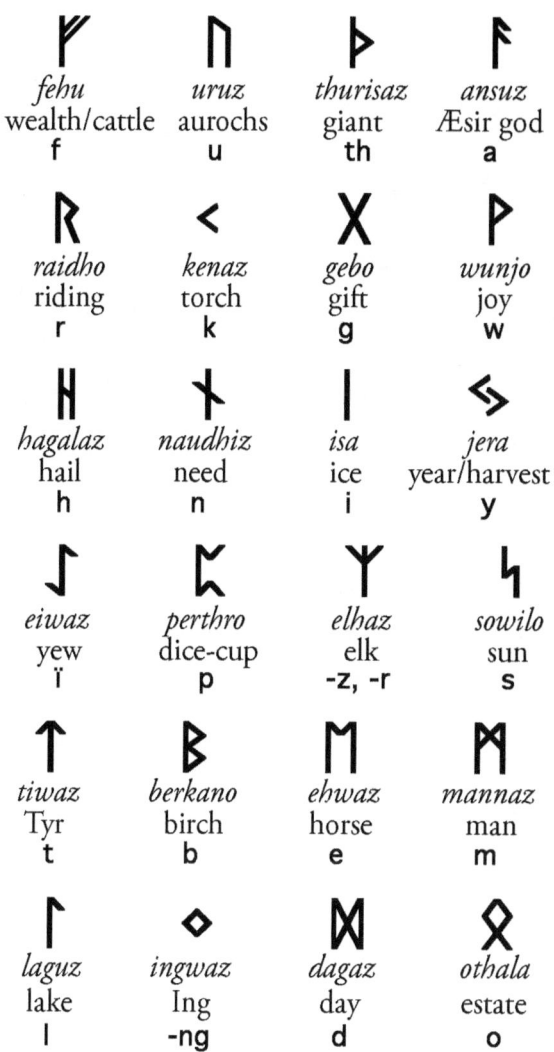

www.ingramcontent.com/pod-product-compliance
Lightning Source LLC
Chambersburg PA
CBHW061253040426
42444CB00010B/2372